Manipulation

HOW TO RECOGNIZE AND OUTWIT EMOTIONAL MANIPULATION AND MIND CONTROL IN YOUR RELATIONSHIPS

2ND EDITION

SARAH NIELSEN

Table of Contents

Introduction	1
Chapter One – Warning Signs	2
Chapter Two – What Makes You a Target	11
Chapter Three – How To Resist Manipulators	18
Chapter Four – Defending Yourself Against Manipulators	26
Chapter Five – Recognizing a Manipulative Relationship	35
Chapter Six – Dealing with Manipulation in a Relationship	50
Chapter Seven – Raising your Self-Esteem Levels	56
Chapter Eight – Following Through with Getting Rid of a Manipulator	61
Conclusion	65

Introduction

It happens too often. People who are suffering from a low self-esteem end up getting stuck in a relationship where they're being controlled by their significant other or even a child. They're the unwitting targets of people who suffer from psychological disorders or emotional disorders that propel them to behave in a manipulative way.

Manipulators have a few main motivations that may be shocking to those being victimized.

They:

- Must advance their purpose and personal gain at the cost of others.

- Are power hungry and need to feel superior in a relationship.

- Are control freaks and need to feel as if they are the dominant one in a relationship at all times.

- Have a low self-esteem and must have power over another in order to raise their perception of themselves.

- See manipulation as merely a game due to a psychopathic tendency.

If you find that you know someone like this, be aware of their actions and yours. Read further to figure out the warning signs of a manipulator and how to deal with one in your relationship.

Chapter One – Warning Signs

You've most likely picked up this book because you feel that you're already emotionally manipulated, or perhaps you're curious as to whether or not you're an emotional manipulator. Believe it or not, you can be a manipulator without being conscious of the act. You may believe that what you're doing is for the better of a relationship, but in all reality, it's not.

Here are the signs of an emotional manipulator, whether you are one or trying to figure out if you're *with* one.

Positive Reinforcement

If you're with a manipulator, they will use positive reinforcement in order to get you to do what they want. For example, they will:

- give you superficial sympathy when something has happened
- use superficial charm
- apologize excessively
- use money, gifts, and approval to get what they want
- use a forced smile or laugh to elicit a positive reaction

Negative Reinforcement

Negative reinforcement is removing someone from a negative situation in order to get what they want. For example, your significant other may say: "You won't have to do the laundry if you fix the sink."

Intermittent Reinforcement

This is when you only sometimes get what you want. It's akin to gambling. You know that you sometimes get a really great response if you do the dishes, so you do the dishes all the time. However, you don't get praise for it all the time, so it's a lot like playing the lottery. One night you might get really great positive reinforcement for doing the dishes, and the next you get the cold shoulder. Yet that small taste of really great positive reinforcement keeps you wanting more, so you keep trying.

Punishment

People who are trying to emotionally manipulate you into doing something for them will use punishment if you do not seem to respond well to the aforementioned ways. These punishments may include some of the following:

- yelling
- silent treatment
- nagging
- intimidation
- emotional blackmail
- threats
- swearing
- sulking
- crying

- playing the victim
- using guilt trips

Traumatic One-Trial Learning

You have one chance to make this person feel better or you're in for a whopping punishment. These experiences are used to teach you that you're not the dominant person in the relationship, and you are expected to be trained to avoid all situations that might upset them in the future. This helps them use more subtle approaches that you're not aware of beyond this point.

Lying

It's hard to catch someone in the act of lying, but if you do, don't sweep it under the rug. Lying in a relationship is very dangerous and is an indication that something is amiss. One of the ways you can minimize your risk of being lied to is to understand that there are people out there that are psychopaths. They lie all the time.

In addition, remembering that lying by omission is still a form of lying. It's very subtle, but don't underestimate the power of it.

Denial

You will never hear of a manipulator admitting they did something wrong. Whatever has happened will always be someone else's fault. They're very good at playing the blame game.

Rationalization

This is an excuse that's made for inappropriate behavior. Don't underestimate how good manipulators are at rationalization. They can rationalize their way out of almost any situation. After all, Ted Bundy rationalized his way out of jail, not once, but twice.

Minimization

Manipulators will play everything down as a joke or make it seem like the situation was not as bad as it was. For instance, a manipulator may do something awful to a coworker and claim that it was all just supposed to be a joke. In reality, they were aiming to hurt that person.

Diversion and Evasion

Manipulators use diversion tactics such as, not giving a straight answer or steering the conversation to another topic. They will evade by being rambling, vague, or irrelevant during a conversation.

Guilt Trips

Guilt is their primary weapon. You can never do anything right with an emotional manipulator because they are always looking for a way to make you feel guilty. Your guilt gains them sympathy, which means they end up getting what they want eventually.

For example, your significant other or friend tells you they got in a fight with their mother about how they don't want to go to a certain college, and now she won't pay for them to go to that college. In reality, there wasn't a fight about the college or even a fight at all. An emotional manipulator will make you feel like you have to be the hero, and you might end up giving them the money for tuition when it's money for something else altogether.

Beware of those who will not fight their own battles and take care of themselves.

Playing the Victim

Have you ever meant someone who seems to always having a problem worse than yours? Whenever you try to tell them something, they either have experienced it or what they're feeling is worse than what you're feeling. They have a way of derailing the conversation and putting the spotlight right back on them.

For example, you tell someone you have a headache. They tell you they have a migraine and feign being very sick. Worse yet, they'll tell you about a time where they had a headache so bad they thought they had a brain tumor. This is emotional manipulation to make you constantly feel for them rather than for yourself.

If you call them on this behavior, they will claim you're selfish and you always want to be in the spotlight.

Seduction

One of the easiest traps to fall into is the seduction trap. A manipulator will use praise, charm, flattery, and support of others in order to gain loyalty and trust. They will offer help just to get into someone's circle so that they can use more subtle tactics.

Projecting Blame

Manipulators will make it look like the victim is the one to blame rather than them. They will tell a lie in order to be able to tell a more believing lie in the future. They will claim the victim is the one being abusive rather than the other way around and it's not beyond them to claim the victim is crazy.

Feigning Confusion

They will try to play dumb when they are accused of doing something and they will act confused when something of importance is brought to their attention, such as a lie they told. Then the manipulator will confuse the victim so that the victim doubts their own perception and eventually believes what the manipulator is telling them. This is another way to make the victim into the 'bad guy'.

Brandishing Anger

It's not that the manipulator is actually angry, but they use anger as a way to get what they want. They will throw irate fits and cry uncontrollably, only to use threats such as calling the police to report abuse. This is all used to put the victim in their place as the submissive.

They Hate Your Honesty

Someone who is trying to manipulate you will not appreciate your honesty, and it won't help in this situation. They're not in the relationship to be a couple. The relationship is all about them and their needs, not yours.

For example, your significant other has forgotten about your birthday. You try to be honest with them and tell them this has hurt you, but instead of apologizing, an emotional manipulator will tell you a lie in order to make *you* feel bad. Your significant other might say something like: "I was going through a really tough time at work today because Kathy lost her husband. She was crying uncontrollably and I had to console her, and you want me to remember to drive to the store to get you a gift? But you're right; I should have remembered your birthday. I'm sorry."

At this point, you realize that they're not really sorry at all, and you may even see real tears in their eyes. However, the story just told was a lie and you end having to console this person rather than make them admitting they conveniently forgot your birthday.

If you see any of these traits with your significant other or a friend, you are dealing with a manipulator. Be aware of their tactics and seek guidance from friends, family, and a psychologist if necessary. One of the important parts to remember about manipulation is that somehow you have made yourself a target. What makes people a target is discussed in Chapter Two.

Types of Manipulators

As most of you are aware of manipulation is a form of deceit. Manipulators are the people who use deceptive tactics to get what they want. Manipulators are not worried about how their manipulation will affect you; all they care about is getting the results that they want. Knowing the warning signs is a start, but knowing the type of emotional manipulator you are dealing with can also help you in defending yourself against them and their deceptive tactics.

Indifferent

This person is the one that acts like they don't care, they seem indifferent towards anything you are doing or saying. In acting indifferent they have actually caught your attention and you are going to try your hardest to break through to them. The more indifferent they act, the more questions you are going to ask because you genuinely care. However, when you start asking questions that is when the manipulation is beginning. Without them having to do or say anything out loud they are able to make you feel sorry for them. And once you start feeling sorry for them you do whatever you can to make them feel better.

Poor Me

This person is probably the most easiest to spot out of all of the emotional manipulators, but that doesn't mean we don't still fall for it time and time again. The poor me manipulators use sympathy and guilt as a way to make you feel sorry for them to get what they want. It is simply human nature to feel for people who are struggling through something or who are facing something different than we are. We react by doing what we can to help them out, so we tend to cater to their demands without realizing we are being manipulated.

Critic

This type of emotional manipulator is a bet more aggressive than the first two types. And while it might be easy to spot what they are doing, many of us who fall victim to manipulators are helpless to stop it, unless we work on improving our mindset and using anti-manipulation techniques. The critic uses criticism as a way to get what they want. The critic constantly criticizes their victim, making them feel like they are not good enough nor will they ever be good enough. Through manipulation the critic makes you feel like you are worthless and they are better than you.

Intimidators

These manipulators are the worst of the worst, they are even more aggressive than the critic. Critics often use intimidation as a way to manipulate you, but intimidators take it a bit further. These types of manipulators use fear rather than criticism to get what they want. They do everything they can to make you afraid of them and once we are afraid of somebody we tend to give in to their demands. Nobody dares stand up to a person who uses fear to manipulate them because they are literally afraid of what that person might physically do.

Chapter Two – What Makes You a Target

Unfortunately, somehow you may have made yourself a target for those who are looking to emotionally manipulate another person. There were warning signs or triggers that they saw in you that made them realize they could be successful. After all, why would they go after someone they knew they couldn't emotionally exploit?

Don't worry, there are ways you can recognize these traits in you and fix them. But first, let's go over them so that you know what to keep an eye out for in your behavior.

What to Look out For in Yourself

These are some things that you should be aware of in yourself so that you can tell if you are a victim of manipulation. If you feel that you have any of these symptoms, you should refer to Chapter Four for tips on how to boost your self-esteem.

The Disease to Please

Do you find that you are always trying to make others happy? Perhaps you are always trying to please your friends, boss, family, or coworkers and nothing ever seems to be enough. You're afraid of conflict and try to avoid it at all costs.

Addiction to Earning Approval

This is a lot like the disease to please, but a little different. Rather than just trying to make others happy, you actually need their approval in order for you to feel good about yourself. Do you go out of the way to ask others how they feel about what you did? Are you always looking for signs that you've done something to displease someone? These are signs that you're looking for approval from others, which is a sure sign that you have a low self-esteem.

Emetophobia

This is actually a fear of negative emotions. You're afraid of showing any anger, disapproval or frustration and are always trying to look like nothing upsets you.

Lack of Assertiveness

Do you have problems saying no to others? Even if it inconveniences you greatly or puts someone else you care about at risk of being disappointed? This is the personality of someone who is naturally submissive, and it's not good for your inner health.

Naiveté

This is very hard to recognize in yourself, but do you feel that no one is ever all that bad? There's always a little bit of good in someone? Perhaps you're being victimized at the moment but you believe that you're really not, despite the warning signs.

Over-Conscientiousness

You may be willing to give someone the benefit of the doubt and see their side of things a little too often. It's okay to be able to put yourself in someone else's shoes, but if they're hurting you in some way, that is wrong.

Low Self-Confidence

Do you find that you're always on the defensive? You may be suffering from low self-confidence because you care too much about what others think of you. For example, someone makes light of your shoes not matching at work one day and you overreact by crying and acting as if that person deliberately tried to emotionally hurt you.

Over-Intellectualization

Perhaps you want to believe the person has a reason for what they're doing. Maybe you, on some level, deserve to be treated the way you are because something bad happened to the other person in their past.

Emotional Dependency

If you rely on others' happiness for your own happiness, you are emotionally dependent. Do not fall into the trap of believing that if your spouse or significant other is not happy, then you can't be happy, too. This is a good way to attract emotional manipulators because your behavior is exactly what they want. They want you to be dependent on them for your happiness and joy.

What Emotional Manipulators Are Looking For

This is a list of the following traits emotional manipulators are looking for in their victims.

- Dependency: They want someone who will depend on them for emotional support, and eventually financial support. They want you to depend on them for your livelihood because this will ensure you will never want to leave.

- Immaturity: People who are immature are easily manipulated because they are either trying to please or they are trying to get back at a caregiver, and thus will do anything.

- Naiveté: People who are naïve believe there is no evil in the world and if there is, it won't touch them.

- Impressionable: This goes along with immaturity. Those who are impressionable are easily swayed to believe something that is not true.

- Trusting: Someone can be too trusting when it comes to others. They believe that everyone has their best interest in mind and cannot believe that others would do something wrong.

- Lonely: Loneliness is a dangerous emotion. It makes humans do anything in order to get rid of it, and that may include allowing a manipulator to come into their life.

- Narcissistic: Manipulators do not always use 'bad' tactics to get what they want. Sometimes they are able to play to people's narcissistic side and flatter them into behaving the way the manipulator wishes.

- Impulsive: Those who are impulsive are not in control of their emotions, which makes them a better target.

- Altruistic: This is the opposite of a psychopath. It's someone who is too honest, too fair, or too empathetic. They always can see how someone else is feeling and they're more easily manipulated by false emotions displayed such as anger and hurt.

- Masochistic: Masochism is believing that you deserve to be punished for something.

If you display any of these tendencies, you should seek a therapist in order to discuss how to get to the root of the situation better. Often times, there are deeply rooted psychological issues that need to be explored in victims of manipulators.

Making Yourself a Hard Target

As you might have guessed based off what you have already read manipulators tend to look for the easy targets. They want to find somebody that they can control and bend to suit their every need. Manipulators almost have some kind of sixth sense that allows them to single out the people that make the best targets.

Now even though you might demonstrate some of the characteristics that make you an ideal target for manipulators that doesn't mean that you can't change. Simply by taking the steps to read this book you have more than proven to yourself that you are ready for a change, you want to break free of this vicious cycle of manipulation. Breaking free is one thing, but you will also need to make some other lifestyle changes to make yourself a harder target for manipulators. After all, nothing would be worse than getting rid of one manipulator only to get hooked in by another.

Avoidance

Honestly, this is probably the simplest tactic you can use to make yourself a hard target for manipulators, simply stay away from them. Now as easy as this might sound to some of you, for others it isn't so cut and dry. Knowing the signs of a manipulator is probably the best way to avoid them, so make sure you brush up the most obvious signs. However, if you do find yourself around a manipulative person your best bet is to not be offended so easily by the things that they do, don't fall victim to their exploitations.

Good Defense

One of the best ways to harden yourself against manipulators is to put up a good defense. In order to build a good defense though you are going to have to have a very good understanding of yourself, including your personality and habits. Self-awareness goes a long way towards scaring off manipulators because they are looking for the weaker people, the ones who will never see them coming. Learning about yourself, including your weaknesses will help you become aware of what you need to protect. Manipulators will play on your weaknesses, but if you know what they are the chance of the manipulator zeroing in on them undetected is lower. Not to mention that the more you know about yourself the better you will be at making decisions about what will benefit you.

Heeding Desires and Fears

Much like a manipulator will pick up on weaknesses, they will also zero in on your inner most desires and fears. Many manipulators, well at least your really good ones, will promise you something that will help you solve a variety of things in life. Whether it is the promise to go on a lavish vacation you can't afford on your own or something even more complex, manipulators know how to dangle that carrot stick to reel you in. They play on fears the same way they do desires; they offer the promise of protection. Knowing and understanding your fears and desires, plus having a solid handle on the reality of them will make you less of a target for manipulators. The best way to do this is to simply face them head on and honestly evaluate them, this takes away any kind of sway anybody could hold over you.

Most of what will help make you a harder target for manipulators is knowing and understanding your weaknesses. Once you have a handle on your weaknesses you can start to take the necessary steps to effectively deal with them, which can include eliminating them from your life. While this might sound easy for some of you, but for others it might sound like the hardest thing in the world. After all, looking into yourself and coming face to face with your weaknesses is something that you have been avoiding for years.

For those of you who are not sure where to start there are numerous self-assessment resources available online. These self-assessments can help you determine what your weaknesses are, which the sooner you know what they are the sooner you can get started on protecting them from manipulators.

Chapter Three – How To Resist Manipulators

Let's face it all of us at some point in our lives have falling victim to manipulators, whether we meant to or not. Falling victim to anything isn't fun, but falling victim to manipulators can be very detrimental to your mental health. Manipulation, whether it is consciously done or not, has devastating effects on a person's emotional health as it makes you start to feel and act like a victim. The problem with manipulation is the longer it goes on the worse you start to feel about yourself. And, the longer the behavior goes on the harder it is for you to escape it.

So how do you go about resisting manipulation you ask? Here are seven simple steps that you can insert into your daily life to help protect you from falling victim to manipulators.

Step one: Give Yourself Some Time

When dealing with manipulators one of the best things that you can do is to give yourself some time before you respond. Manipulators will often make demands and expect you to respond right away, which is when you are more likely to make a response based on emotion rather than logic. Manipulators will go so far as to pressure you into giving them a response right away, so hold your ground. No matter what you do, do NOT ask permission in any way, shape, or form.

By giving yourself sometime between their request and your response you are able to look at everything that is going on. You can sit and think through all of your options logically rather than emotionally. Not only that but you will feel a sense of control, which is vital to helping to boost up your self-confidence again.

Step Two: Don't Explain Yourself

Now one thing that is very important to resisting manipulation is to not fall into the manipulators trap. No matter how tempting it might be for you, do NOT explain to the manipulator why you need to take some time to think about your response. It is none of their business or concern, even if they pretend like it is, why you want to think things through. Do not tell them what you are going to be thinking over or even when will respond to them. If you do this you are simply falling into the manipulators clutches once again. You can acknowledge the fact that you heard what they asked, but do not explain yourself, keep it simple and to the point.

Step Three: Desensitize Yourself

this is probably one of the hardest steps you will have to take to learn how to resist manipulation. Manipulators play on your emotions, they learn what buttons they can push to get you to do the things that they want. They know pushing those buttons will get them their way because you don't want to upset people or you will feel guilty if you say no t helping somebody. Manipulators play on your guilt, fear, and your anxiety. What you need to do to resist them is to desensitize yourself, you need to learn how to cope with uncomfortable feelings, such as how you feel when you tell somebody no. The better you can cope with those feelings the easier it will be to resist manipulation in the long run.

Step Four: Call It What It Is

One of the reasons why manipulation is so powerful is because victims don't call it what it is. Instead they silently endure the manipulation and go about living their life. It's how the pattern gets started. The longer you stay quiet about the manipulation the longer it will go on. To resist manipulation you have to call it for what it is. Simple let the manipulator know that you know what they are doing, tell them they are manipulating you and it won't work any longer. The sooner you call it what it is, the sooner you can shift the power into your hands.

Step Five: Stopping the Manipulation

In order to resist manipulation you have to stop the manipulation in its track. The best way to do this is to tell the manipulator that you know what they are trying to do. You need to further explain to them that the tactics they are trying to use to get you to do what they want is not going to work. Being upfront about it goes a long way towards stopping it.

Step Six: You Call The Shots

One of the most important things you can do to help resist manipulation is to start calling the shots, you need to set your own terms and then stick with them. To do this you are going to have to assert your intention, you tell the manipulator what it is you are going to be doing. You need to instill in the manipulator how you want to be treated.

A big part of calling the shots is setting boundaries with the manipulator. When setting boundaries you need to make the boundaries clear, plus you need to make it clear what will happen if those boundaries are crossed. Setting limits also goes along with creating boundaries. Be clear in setting your limits and be clear in what happens if the limits are reached. Doing all of this will allow you to take back control of your life from the manipulator. You need to clearly state to the manipulator that you are a person and should be respected. Tell them, even if they might not understand, that even if you and they have differencing opinions or values that isn't a bad thing nor is it wrong. Just remember you can tell them all of this, but you cannot make them listen. You also need to learn when to just walk away.

Step Seven: Compromise

Now honestly this is going to be all on you because manipulators do not know or understand how to compromise with others, nor are they usually willing to compromise. Manipulators simply want what they want when they want it and will do everything in their power to get it. However, when it comes to meeting your own needs you need to be willing to compromise ad negotiate with yourself, you need to determine what is most important for you, as well as what you strongly desire.

So, knowing that manipulation is emotionally harmful is one thing, doing something about it is another. Most people who fall victim to manipulation have no idea that there are certain things that they can do to resist the manipulation. If you are tired of being manipulated you no longer have to sit back and allow it to continuously happen. You can stand up against the manipulators and begin to take your life back.

Knowing how to resist manipulation is one thing, but putting it to work is another matter entirely. What you need to keep in mind is that no matter how long you have been manipulated there is always the fact that you can take your life back; you can stand up and regain control. However, standing up and taking back your life is not going to happen overnight, even if you use the steps above to resist further manipulation. What you need to do is work on it every day, sometimes you are going to fall back a step or two, but don't let that discourage you. It is only going to be with time and effort that you are able to break the viscous cycle of manipulation that you have been living in.

Tips for Resisting Manipulators

Knowing the steps you need to take to resist manipulators is helpful, but sometimes we can't always follow those steps. Or in some cases we follow all of these steps and still find ourselves having problems resisting them. Luckily, there are a few others things that you can try to help build your resistance to manipulators.

- If the person simply won't take no for an answer you need to be prepared to stand your ground. During the course of the conversation they are going to do whatever they can to get you to change your mind, they will even say things that might make you feel guilty. However, the worst thing you can do is give in to them because that means that they have won. Instead of giving in you need to learn to let the things they say slide off your back. No matter how inflammatory something might be just learn to let it go. If you don't react to it, they can't use it against you to get what they want.

- Sometimes the best way to resist a manipulator is to simply walk away from them. In some cases though that isn't always possible. If you can't just walk away from them, the best you can do is to limit just how much time you are spending with them. In all honesty, the less you are around them the fewer chances they are going to have to manipulate you.

- Another great way to resist manipulation is to agree with everything that person is saying. No matter what reason they might give you to try and persuade you to change your mind you need to agree with them. Even if they are attacking you, by agreeing with them you are cutting off their arguments one at a time. You don't have to agree with everything they are saying, you can also agree with part of what they are saying. You can also just agree that they have the right to their opinion. No matter how you agree with them it will throw them off guard and help you in standing your ground.

- Sometimes the only way you are going to be able to resist manipulators is to stand your ground. Do not budge from your original position, which can be harder than it sounds. Manipulators are known for not giving up until they get their way, so they are going to throw everything they can at you. Standing your ground is often going to require you repeating yourself until the manipulator backs off. For each argument they give you simply tell them you understand what they are saying but you are not going to do it.

- One thing that you need to realize with emotional manipulators is that you probably can't change them, so there really is no point in trying. Something else to think about with manipulators is that when you are dealing with them do not let your emotions get in the way. Emotional arguments are only going to cause manipulation levels to rise. Your best bet at putting up any kind of resistance is to stick strictly to the facts.

- When it comes to dealing with a manipulator you need to know beforehand that no matter what happens the manipulator is not going to let you "win" the argument. A manipulator will never concede that you are right or that they are wrong. Knowing this can help end any kind of discussion before stuff gets out of hand. Not only that but if you try and defend yourself to a manipulator it is not going to work. Everything that you say will simply be falling onto deaf ears.

- Something that you really need to focus on when resisting manipulators is your weaknesses. The more that you know and understand about your own weaknesses the better. Manipulators will use your weaknesses against you in an attempt to get you to see things their way. Knowing what your weaknesses are can help you protect yourself when confronted by a manipulator. Knowing what causes you to give into somebody even when you don't want to can also help you resist manipulation.

- When it comes to resisting manipulation the best thing you can possibly do is stop the manipulator in their tracks. The longer you allow the manipulator to continue the higher your risk for giving in. By cutting it short you reduce the risk of you caving in to their demands. To keep it short, set your boundaries and stick to them. Keep all of your responses short and to the point, using only the facts. If that doesn't work you might just simply have to walk away from the conversation.

- When dealing with a manipulator do not take their threats personally. They only reason they are using any kind of threat is to try and get you to give in to their demands. If you know what they are trying to do it can help you resist them. Plus in some cases you can even call the manipulator out on the carpet. As long as you know it won't make the situation worse, you can tell the person that you know exactly what they are doping and it won't work.

No matter how you decide to resist manipulation you need to realize it is not going to come easy at first. You have spent so long being manipulated by people that it is pretty much second nature for you to give in to others. It is going to take to learn how to use these methods correctly, so don't become discouraged if things don't always work out as you planned. No matter what tools you employ in your fight to resist manipulation it is going to require strength on your end, you have to build up your mental and emotional mindset to be able to successfully resist manipulation. Doing this requires you to become stronger than you were before; you need to firmly believe in who you are and what you believe in.

Chapter Four – Defending Yourself Against Manipulators

After reading this far you have a pretty good understanding of what manipulation is and how it works. You should also have a better understanding of the warning signs of manipulators, as well as how they pick out their targets. Learning how to harden yourself against manipulation is great way to prevent yourself from becoming a victim in the future, but it is not going to help you in your current situation.

If you are reading this book right now, chances are you are dealing with at least one manipulator in your life and you are sick of being walked all over. You are ready to stand up for yourself and regain control of your life back, but the problem is you don't know how to do it. Learning how to resist manipulation is a good start, but you must also learn how to defend yourself against manipulators.

If you are ready to learn how to defend yourself against manipulators, which you must be if you made it this far, here are several steps that you can follow to ensure you are successful.

Step One: Be Aware

In order to take action of any kind, no matter what the situation might be, you have to first be aware of what you are looking at. In other words if you want to defend yourself against manipulators you have to be able to recognize the people that are manipulating you. One of the biggest problems with recognizing manipulators is how subtle they are, it's not like they advertise that they are using manipulation. Earlier in this book we told you about the warning signs of manipulators, as well as what manipulators look for in a target. Use what you have learned to start recognizing the manipulators in your life. Once you know who they are you can start working on defending yourself with the following actions.

Step Two: Realize It's Not Personal

Now this statement is not entirely true, how true it is will actually depend on the manipulator. However, in general most manipulators are not looking to personally harm you, they are simply more concerned with getting what they want and will do whatever it takes to get it. In majority of cases you are simply in the manipulators way, so they will do what they can, even if it means make you feel bad, to get you to give them what they want. You need to remember that it's their choice as a person how they act; you cannot control their choices or actions.

Step Three: Give Yourself Some Space

One of the best things you can do with manipulators is to give yourself some space from them. In other words do everything that you can to stay away from them. Now, honestly, sometimes this is easier said than done, especially if the manipulator is somebody close to you, such as a family member or even a spouse. If you aren't willing or ready to say good bye to the manipulator you will simply have to learn how to effectively deal with them.

Step Four: Work on Improving Your Mind

Now no matter how much you might want to you seriously cannot spend all of your time and energy on running away from manipulative people. And, while it is best to avoid them, the problem is you attracted them at one point, so unless you change some things about yourself you are going to keep attracting them. To truly defend yourself against manipulators you need to work on improving your mindset. Tips for improving your mindset can be found at the end of this chapter.

Step Five: Learn Anti-Manipulation Techniques

Once you have a strong mindset you are not going to need this step, but until then you will want to learn and adopt several anti-manipulation techniques, which these techniques can be found further on in this chapter. Before you start using the techniques though you will want to practice them, which we recommend doing so with somebody you trust. The more you practice these techniques the better you will be able to respond when facing the problem in your daily life.

Step Six: Be Direct

manipulators act the way they do to get the things that they want, while subtly might be their gamer you do not have to take any part in that. Instead of being subtle be very direct with manipulators. If somebody is trying to manipulate you into doing something don't play their game, simply come out and ask them what it is they want. If you are going to go this route make sure that you listen to what it is they have to say and do not judge them. In some cases simply doing that shows the manipulator there is a different way they can go about getting the things they want.

Step Seven: Be Consistent

Now once you have started to defend yourself against manipulators you need to keep doing so, you must be consistent. If you are not being consistent you are going to end up sending mixed signals, which will encourage manipulators to continue acting the way they do. Pick a method that you feel will work best, whether it is an anti-manipulation technique or being direct, and then stick with that method until they no longer are trying to manipulate you. However, be prepared in the beginning for a strong attack from the manipulators, as they will try harder when you first start standing up to them.

Step Eight: Leave

Sometimes no matter how hard you try or how consistent you are people are still going to continue to try and manipulate you. If this is the case the best thing you can do is just walk away from that person. It might be hard, but you need to put yourself first. Accepting manipulating behavior will do nothing but destroy your mental and emotional health.

Tips For Adopting an Anti-Manipulation Mindset

One of the most important lessons you will ever learn when it comes to manipulation is that nobody can manipulate you if you don't let them. If you allow somebody to manipulate you that means you have giving them control over you, whether you did it willingly or subconsciously.

Using anti-manipulation techniques is a great way to defend yourself against those that are manipulating you, but the techniques are not going to be very effective if you don't have the right state of mind. Your current state of mind is obviously not very good, as it is what is allowing people to manipulate you. What you need to do is change the way you think, adopt different beliefs and a new attitude.

So, how do you change the way you think? Here are some tips that you will find quite useful.

- Take Responsibility of Your Feelings – You are the only person who creates your feelings; what other people do or say doesn't create those feeling it just triggers things. Your feelings are determined by your state of mind, as well as your attitude and beliefs based on the situation you are facing. Taking responsibility of your feelings helps improve your mindset because you are taking control; you are not giving the control over to those that are manipulating you. The more you practice the better you will become at choosing how you are feeling.

- Ignore Guilt –You can only be responsible for your own feelings; you cannot be responsible for how other people feel. How you create your own feelings, the same holds true for them. Manipulators often use guilt as a way to get the things that they want. You need to learn to ignore any guilt trips that are being placed on you. If they feel sad or mad or whatever they tell you they will feel, that is their problem and doing, not yours. The same thing holds true for actions, you cannot take responsibility for what others do; you can only be responsible for yourself.

- Don't Feel Fear – This one kind of follows the same line as guilt. Manipulators use it to gain control over you, they often try and exploit your fears for their own personal gain. What you need to do is learn how to face your fears and overcome. After all if you aren't afraid of something, such as losing your job, then the manipulator can't threaten you with that fear to make you do what they want. Now we know that getting over your fear is nowhere near as easy as it sounds. You will have to do it one day at a time, but each time your fear pops up you need to acknowledge it; this will eventually help you come to terms with it.

- Let go of pain – Old pain is a manipulators pot of gold and sadly we all seem to have some old pain buried deep inside. If you have any old pain buried deep inside you, you know the one thing that you avoid thinking about at all costs, you need to let go of that pain. If you can't do it on your own you can always seek the help and guidance of a licensed therapist.

- Love yourself – We all know that people with low-self-esteem make the best targets for any kind of predator, which includes manipulators. Manipulators use what you least like about yourself and exploit that to get what they want. What you need to do is learn to love yourself for who you are, accept the god with the bad and don't let things bother you so much. If you are happy with who you are, nobody can use anything against you. There are many self-improvement techniques that you can use to help improve your self-confidence, as well as your self-esteem.

- Detach yourself – You cannot identify yourself as belonging to something. For example, you are not your job. If you feel like you are your job you are going to naturally feel fear over losing it, which manipulators can use to their advantage. What you need to do is detach yourself from those things you identify with. You need to remember that you are simply you; you cannot be any more or any less. Things don't define who you are, you define who you are.

Anti-Manipulation Techniques You Can Use

Once you get yourself in the right frame of mind you are ready to start practicing some anti-manipulation techniques. The great thing about these techniques is they are perfect to use when you need to defend yourself against manipulation. However, in order for them to work properly you have to be in the right frame of mind, so get your head together before you start working on these.

Translator

This anti-manipulation technique is probably the easiest to learn and carry out, but it also happens to be the most effective. How this method works is you flip things around on your manipulator. When you are in a scenario where you are being manipulated by somebody what you need to do is sum up what they are asking in a simple sentence. Then simply ask them if this is what they want. This is a very direct method and puts all of the cards out on the table.

This is the best method that you can use to really find out what the other person is feeling or thinking. The problem with people today is that most people aren't very direct; they don't really say what it is they want or need; they do things in a roundabout way. The translator method is perfect in solving these issues because you will be able to clarify things and get stuff out in the open.

Literal

This method deals with the subtext of a conversation just like the translator method does, but in a rather different way. The translator method relies on putting things out in the open, but the literal method involves ignoring the subtext. If somebody is beating around the bush and you are picking up the cues, simple ignore it and move on. This method is perfect when you know that people are trying to manipulate you. It is also great when dealing with people who are not as important to you.

One of the greatest things about this method is that it is very logical. It is based on the fact people should ask for what it is they want. If they don't bother to ask then they really don't deserve to have it. This method is all about straight talk, if you don't say it, it literally doesn't exist. Just keep in mind this method requires you to deal with a lot of pressure, so be prepared to handle it.

Subtext Exaggeration

This method is similar to the literal method, but instead of ignoring the subtext, you simply react to just that. You ignore everything that is being said and only respond to the subtext. However, you don't just simply respond to it, you need to really push things over the top. You need to exaggerate your actions when you respond to the subtext. If somebody is trying to manipulate you into going somewhere, respond with what you think they would say. Yes I am a bad person for breaking your heart. Just remember that no matter what you say no actions are needed, you are not going to go where they want or do what they want, and you need to ignore that part as well.

The subtext exaggeration method is one of the best ones to use when you know 100% without a doubt that people are trying to manipulate you. This method allows you to make it perfectly clear to that person that you know they are trying to manipulate you and that it isn't going to work, no matter what they might try. In order for this method to be effective you need to be able to quickly read the subtext because you have to respond to it in a quick manner.

Time Delay

Time delay is best used when you know without a doubt that you are being manipulated, but you don't know exactly how they are manipulating you. This is often used when you can't read the subtle messages a person is giving off or when you just aren't sure what a person is asking. If you feel uncomfortable about anything or feel like you are being [pressured into making a decision you need to delay in making that decision.

With time delay what is important is that you tell them that as soon as you make up your mind you will let them know. Doing so puts you in charge, not them. Not to mention doing it this way makes it to where they have no use in pestering you about the original topic. Being that they are manipulators they will most likely bring it up again, what you need to do is stick to your guns and remind them that you will let them know what you decide once you have made up your mind. People who are dealing with a weak state of mind or who feel like they are going to give in to somebody's demands will find this to be a very useful method. It can also be used as an emergency method while you work on improving your state of mind.

Chapter Five – Recognizing a Manipulative Relationship

Now just because you know and understand what the warning signs are in terms of a manipulative person that doesn't mean you aren't still involved in a manipulative relationship. Sadly, every day both men and women enter into what they think is going to be the best relationship of their life only to find out too late that the person they are with is more interested in manipulating them than loving them.

Entering into these unhealthy relationships causes the victim to lose themselves. The victim is more interested in pleasing the person they are with; all they care about is making their partner happy. Victims often end up losing family and friends over these manipulative relationships because they don't see the signs until everything is too late. If you have loved ones that are concerned about your relationship, you might want to pay them some mind. And chances are if you are reading this, you have already taken the first step to finding yourself again.

If you are interested in finding yourself again the first thing you will need to do is look closely at your relationship. You need to determine if your relationship is actually taking away from who you are, are you changing because of your relationship for the worst? If you are, you must take the steps necessary to put a stop to things as soon as possible, the longer you wait, the worse things will get.

Step One: Evaluate

When evaluating your relationship you are going to need to look closely at every aspect of it. However, simply looking at it is not going to get you very far if you hide behind omissions and half truths. When evaluating our relationship you have to be 100% honest with yourself. Look at the relationship from the very beginning from an objective stand point, pretend you are on the outside looking in.

Step Two: Is Your Relationship Abusive

Now not all manipulative relationships are going to be considered abusive, but majority of them are in some way or another. You need to ask yourself if you are in an abusive relationship by asking yourself a series of questions about your partner, as well as yourself.

- Does your partner make fun of you in front of your loved ones?

- Does your partner constantly or occasionally put you down or belittle you?

- Does your partner use fear or guilt trips to get you to comply with their wishes?

- Does your partner tell you what you can wear and how to do your hair and makeup?

- Does your partner tell you that you are nothing without them?

- Is your partner rough with you without your consent, such as hitting, shoving, grabbing, etc?

- Check up on you constantly when you are out with friends?

- Blame drugs or alcohol as to why they do or say hurtful things?

- Tell you it's your fault for how they are acting or feeling?

- Stop you from doing things that you want, including keeping you from friends and family?

- Are you worried about how your partner will react or act?

- Do you feel responsible for your partner's feelings?

- Ado you constantly make excuses or apologize for your partner's behavior or actions?

- Think you can make your relationship better if you only changed a few things about yourself?

- Do everything that you can to avoid upsetting your partner?

- Constantly feel that no matter how hard you try, your partner is not happy with you?

- Stay in the relationship because you are afraid of what will happen if you leave?

Now when answering these questions it is VERY important to answer them honestly. You cannot justify your partner's actions or your own actions. You cannot say they only do it sometimes or it has only happened once, you need to simply answer each of the above questions with a straight yes or no. And, if you answer more than just a few questions with a yes, there is no doubt that you are in an abusive relationship, whether it is a physically abusive one or an emotional one.

Step Three: Evaluate Your Other Relationships

Part of determining if you are in a manipulative relationship is looking at the relationships you have with your friends and family. When evaluating these relationships you are going to need to think about how they were before your relationship with your partner started and compare them to how things are now. Some things to look for is how much time are you spending with your friends and family members, as well as how much time you are spending with your partners. Also look at whether or not you are avoiding the people who are about you because of the way your partner treats them or because it is easier to avoid them than to get your partner to hang out with them.

What you need to bear in mind is that if your loved ones are concerned about you or if your partner is pushing your friends and family members away from you, those are not the signs of a healthy relationship. Healthy relationships allow you to bring about the best in each other, not the worst. Again when evaluating your other relationships you have to be honest with yourself, half truths and lies will get you nowhere.

Step Four: Are You Blind to Your Partner's Faults?

Now infatuation is not always a bad thing. In fact, most new relationships have some sort of infatuation going on; if you aren't totally infatuated with your new partner in the beginning you might consider that to be a little strange. While it's great to always want to see our partners in the best light, it can also cause problems because it makes us blind to our partner's true nature. Sometimes we willing brush aside comments from our loved ones that we should actually be paying close attention to because they often have our best interests at heart. Being blinded to your partner's faults can actually prevent you from seeing the early warning signs of a manipulative relationship.

To see if you are blinded to your partner's faults and to see if you should listen a bit more closely to your friends and family's concern, ask yourself these questions.

- Are you becoming defense about your partner's actions?
- Are you constantly apologizing for your partner's behavior?
- Do you get upset when somebody questions your relationship?
- Are you constantly changing your plans to do what your [partner wants?
- Do you always hang out with your partner's friends rather than your own friends?
- Have you replaced your favorite people and places with your partner's favorite friends and places? Or have you replaced them with places and friends you have meet since your relationship started?

If you answered yes to any of these things you are most likely involved in a very manipulative relationship. If the relationship wasn't a manipulative one you would have no need or desire to defend your partner's actions nor would you have any reason to hide what is really going on. By cutting you off from your past all your partner is doing is making themselves the center of your world. By doing this what they have managed to do is eliminate any competition for your attention. Friends and family generally see this sooner than you do, so if they are voicing concerns you need to start listening. If the relationship was a healthy one your loved ones would be supporting you rather than worried about you.

Step Five: Questioning Events

Have you ever talked to your partner's friends about a specific event? I am pretty sure you have, after all, when you are hanging out with people, one thing you tend to do is communicate. Ina normal, healthy relationship talking to your partner's friends doesn't usually raise any red flags, but in a manipulative relationship it often can. Think back to the times where you have talked with your partner's friends about something that you and your partner had also talked about, such as a camping trip they all went on. Do both of the stories match up? Or did talking to your partner's friends cause you to scratch your hand in wonder and think to yourself that wasn't the story you were originally told.

Now honestly, sometimes it is the friends that change the story, but if you are thinking you are in a manipulative relationship, chances are it was your partner not their friends that changed the finer details around. What you need to do is make notes of all of the times things don't add up rather than dismiss the thoughts. Manipulators usually do so through half-truths and omissions rather than lies. Lies are discovered easier and cause you to re-think things faster than a half-truth will. If you notice a lot of half-truths and omissions confront your partner on them, but pay close attention to their reaction. If they get defensive or you simply aren't happy with their answer, you need to rethink your relationship right away. Putting it off and making excuses can lead to disastrous consequences.

Step Six: Keep Your Support System

Manipulators tend to cut you off from everybody that you love and care about. How they go about doing this will depend on the person, but the goal is to make it to where you have no support system so that you must rely 100% on them. Some partners will treat your friends and family horribly in an attempt to drive them away, others will constantly cause drama. Even better are the ones that will create problems and then whine to you about how they are all conspiring against your partner so they have a "valid" reason for not wanting to be around your friends and family. Keeping you away from your support system is done in such a way that it will be your decision to cut them out of your life. Manipulators will work things to paint themselves in the best possible light, so you won't ever think to blame them for your actions.

Step Seven: Recognizing Possessiveness and Jealousy

Everybody wants somebody to love and care about them, as well as protect them. To a certain degree it is actually considered to be something nice. Where you need to start being concerned is if your partner is overly-protective of you. Some signs that they are too protective include constantly asking where you are, checking up on you to see if you are where you said you would be, or questioning you relentlessly if you are home later than you said you would be. Other concerning actions would be your partner trying to make you feel guilty about spending time with friends instead of them, such as saying you obviously don't care about them if you want to hang out with a friend.

Step Eight: Double Standards

One of the most concerning signs of a manipulative relationship is where a partner uses double standards. If your partner says you can't do something, but then they go out and do what they said you can't, that is a double standard and is a big cause for concern. Something else to watch out for is a no-win situation. These are when you get berated by your partner no matter what you do. In these situations no matter what you decide to do you are going to be at fault.

Step Nine: Asking Forgiveness

Now when you do something wrong it is only right to ask for forgiveness, so how does this serve as a warning sign to a manipulative relationship, you ask. The answer is rather easy, manipulative people will constantly ask for forgiveness after making the same mistakes over and over again. They know what they did is wrong, so they beg you to forgive them with the promises that they will change. And while they might sound like they mean it, honestly it is all a big part of control. They use compassion to keep you in the relationship. And all too often what happens is they change for a little bit, just long enough t convince you that things have changed, and then they go out and do the same thing. This vicious circle will eat away at your self-confidence over time, so the sooner you stop it the better.

Step Ten: Forgive Yourself

Now after reading all of this you are probably beating yourself up for falling for a person like that, but don't. The truth is manipulative people portray themselves as great people, and more people than you realize fall for their tricks. On the outside these people appear confident, almost to the point of arrogant, and they are often quite intelligent and talented, so it is easy to see why people would fall for them so quickly. What you need to realize is that these people put up a great front, but for them it's all about the control. They honestly feel like they have to be in control of everything and if they aren't in control they feel that the worst possible things will happen. However, you need to come to terms with the fact that they are using this control to keep you in the relationship. You need to tell yourself that it is not your fault that you love them; it is their fault for using that love as a way to manipulate you.

Getting Out of a Manipulative Relationship

If you have determined that you are in a manipulative relationship one of your best choices is to end the relationship. However, easy as ending the relationship might sound, it is not always the case. Sometimes ending the relationship is even harder than staying in it for a variety of reasons. No matter what reasons you might tell yourself or what reasons your partner might tell you, the only way you are going to be able to move forward with your life is to make a clean break. Ending a manipulative relationship is going to take courage, but once you begin it is important to keep moving forward.

Prepare to End It

The first part of this is the easiest, as the first thing you have to do is admit that you are being manipulated by your partner. Most relationships go on longer than they should because the victim doesn't want to admit that anything is wrong. You have been making excuses for so long about your partner that you have actually started to believe what you are saying. The first thing you must do in order to prepare yourself is to admit that you are being manipulated.

Once you have admitted that there is a problem you can work on why ending the relationship is the best choice for you. You can start to focus on how ending the relationship is actually going to improve your life in the long run. Knowing how it will benefit you and make you happier will also help motivate you to leave. Your best bet is to write down all of the reasons why leaving is the best choice.

Not sure where to get started? Here is a quick look at just a few of the reasons as to why you need to leave the relationship.

- You can be your own person again. You can do the stuff you loved doing before you lost yourself in the relationship.

- You can begin enjoying your friends and family again.

- You will see a huge jump in your self-esteem.

- No more fear and anxiety controlling everything you do.

Once you have made up your mind that leaving is the best thing for you, you need to figure out what you are going to say to your partner. You don't want to wing it because that leaves you open to their manipulation. When coming up with what you plan to say keep it short and to the point. You don't need to go into tons of details, the more you talk the more room they have to make empty promises. More importantly don't be vindictive, stay calm as you tell them that it is over. If you start acting emotional in front of them you are opening up the conversation for further manipulation. To help ensure everything goes smoothly find a trusted friend or family member and practice with them what you are going to say, so that you are 100% comfortable with it. And remember ending it in your mind before you do it in person can make saying what you have to say easier.

Planning what you say is important, but so is how and where you will say it. For example, if you are afraid of how they will react doing it in public rather than private is a better choice. Even better you can simply leave them a note, so you don't have to deal with them face to face. Bear in mind the timing needs to be right as well. Don't end the relationship after the two of you have been out drinking all night, do it when things are a bit more stable to lessen the chance of an emotional response.

Part of planning the end of the relationship involves figuring out how you are going to get your stuff back, whether you were living with your partner or just had stuff at their house. If you are living with the person make sure you have a place to move to before you break it off with your partner. How you get your stuff back will depend on how safe you feel. Some find it easier to sneak the stuff out in small batches, while others find it easier to go back after the break up. No matter how you deice you can always use friends as back up.

Carry Out Your Plan

Now that you know what you need to do; you need to carry out your plan. One thing to keep in mind as you start to carry out your plan is that you need to be firm, you can be nice, but you still have to be firm. No matter what kind of reaction your partner has you need to say what you have to say and leave. Chances are your partner will try and manipulate you anyway by crying about how you never gave them a chance to explain. Don't fall for it though because in reality you have given them far too many chances.

Once you have told your partner what you have to say you need to leave. Do NOT stick around. You don't need to hear what your partner has to say nor do you need to witness the fake tears, no matter how real they might look. You are not here to negotiate with your partner. One way to make things easier is to keep your distance from your partner. When telling them what is on your mind stand or sit as far from them as possible, do NOT let them touch you. If they do touch you, you are at risk for being manipulated back into the relationship. If they do try to hold your hand or lay their hand on your arm, shift away and continue saying what you came to say.

Now remember you are leaving a person, who has spent the entire relationship manipulating you, chances are they aren't going to stop that behavior anytime soon. You need to be on the lookout for that type of behavior. Do not let their emotional outburst change your mind. No matter what they might say or do or how they might act, you must remind yourself that you are leaving the relationship because of that behavior. You can't let it work on you any longer.

Once you have said everything that you came to say you need to turn around and walk away. Do NOT look back, simply hold your head up and walk to your car or your friend's car. And more importantly do not tell your now ex-partner where you plan on going. Even if you think they have an idea of where you will be staying, do not mention or acknowledge it. Frankly, it's none of their concern where you go or what you do from here on out.

Continue To Follow Through With Your Plan

Now that you have broken up with the person, you might think that you are done. Sadly, that is not the case. Now comes something even more important than the actual break up, you must now follow through with your plan. You need to ensure that the break up remains permanent.

Now that you have broken up you need to avoid all contact with that person. Giving them any sort of attention after you have left them, gives them the idea that there is a small chance that you can work things out and get back together. Not to mention when you avoid them you can no longer fall victim to their manipulations. Avoiding all contact means ALL contact, no talking, no Facebooking, nothing. Some exes are going to be more persistent than others, so you might need to invest in a restraining order.

Something that you are going to need to be prepared for is the feeling of loneliness and sadness that will come after the break up. This is when you are going to be the most vulnerable and you will start to question your decision. This is normal, but for those of you who just left a manipulator it is often worse because you also have to work on finding yourself again. Suddenly every aspect of your life is yours to control, it is up to you to make all of the decisions. No matter how low you might get you need to stand by your decision, do not change your mind. Tell yourself everyday that things will get easier; you just need to ride it out. Remember you were fine before the relationship, so you can be fine again.

Tips For Making The Break Up Work

Once you have decided that the break up is for the best and that no matter what you are not going back, your life is going to start to change for the better. Now even though it might start changing for the better that doesn't mean things are going to always be easy. You are going to wake up some mornings really missing your ex. You might even start thinking that you were too hard on them and that they deserve a second chance. Now these feelings are normal and they will eventually go away, but that doesn't make dealing with them any easier.

If you are having a hard time dealing with the break up there are things that can help you get through even the roughest of days. Here are some useful tips that you can immediately put to use.

- Hanging out with your loved ones – Most of us think that after a break up we need to spend all of our time alone, but that is not even close to the truth. In fact, total isolation is the worst thing to do after breaking up with a manipulator. Sure some alone time is good, but leaning on loved ones will help you stay strong and get through even the roughest of days. Remember loved ones are your support system, talk to them about how bad the relationship was and how bad you are feeling. They will be there to help you get through it and the more they know and understand the more they can help.

- Keep busy – One of the worst things you can do is lie around the house feeling sorry for yourself. The more you sit around and do nothing the more likely you are to start thinking that you made a mistake. Plus the more you feel sorry for yourself the harder it will be to get over the relationship. Your best bet is to stay as busy as possible. How you stay busy is entirely up to you, but you can always hang out with friends, work some extra shifts, pick up a hobby, or even head back to school. The important part to staying busy is to get out of the house as much as possible, as isolating yourself inside your home will cause you to really feel alone. Planning your week can also help, especially if you create something that you have to look forward to each day.

- Remind yourself of how much happier you are – Now obviously some days this is going to be more true than others, but over time it will be very easy to see. Every day when you first wake up or even before you go to bed think about one thing that you can now do since you left your ex. Create a list of all of the things that you can do and how much better your life is can also help. It's nice to have the list to look over when you are having those down days.

Chapter Six – Dealing with Manipulation in a Relationship

Sometimes it's not always possible to get out of a relationship with a manipulator, such as a parent/child relationship. In some cases, you may truly care about the person you're with and you want to help them, but don't allow this to become another way for the manipulator to take control. There are ways that you can deal with a manipulator, but it will take some time and some hard work on you.

Focus on You

All too often, victims of manipulators focus on their tormentor rather than themselves. This is exactly what the manipulator wants, which will only make their behavior worse. The reality of the situation is that you can only help yourself and not the person who is manipulating you, so focus on you rather than on them. Sometimes this will actually resolve the situation all on its own because the manipulator will realize they are not in control anymore and leave.

Do not fall into the trap of sharing your emotions and feelings with a manipulator. They will only turn this against you in the end and having them thrown back at you from a different perspective may be very difficult to handle. Remember that manipulators are not susceptible to empathy and will not be able to take your side in the matter.

Assess the Value

Is this relationship really worth all of this effort to you? Sometimes the damage is already so severe and your sense of happiness and integrity has been damaged so badly that you just need to leave the relationship. This is difficult to do if you have a low self-esteem, so be sure to check out Chapter Four on ways to raise your self-esteem levels to be able to face your tormentor and have the courage to stand on your own.

Of course, sometimes it is impossible to get out of a relationship with a manipulator because they may be your child, so you have to assess how the relationship is hurting you as the parent and figure out how to alleviate some of the manipulation. If you are the parent dealing with a manipulative child, sometimes it's best to have that child see a psychologist to get to the root of the issue.

Use Assertiveness

The first step to using assertiveness in a relationship is to take back the control you have. You are most likely very used to complying with your manipulator just to avoid an altercation, but there are other ways to avoid altercations. When one starts to arise and the manipulator starts to do something that upsets you, simply remove yourself from the situation. You can do this by stating, "I need time to think about this."

Do not allow the manipulator to ask you *why* you need time because this is another tactic they use to regain control! Simply restate the previous statement over and over again until you are out of the situation, in another room, outside, or in another location completely.

Once you're removed from the situation, you must confront your fears and anxieties that are building up. Why do you feel guilty when the manipulator uses this tactic? This is very hard to do, but there must be a reason as to why you are responding the way you are, being submissive and being the victim. This may be a great challenge for you, but it could save your relationship or set you up for healthier ones in the future.

Finally, in a calmed state, confront the manipulator and tell them exactly what you just learned about yourself. For example, they may threaten to leave you during an argument and that makes you feel afraid. Simply state that to the manipulator and tell them that if they state what they want with respect, you might be more willing to listen. Then tell them firmly, but not without control, that you will not allow them to play on your fears any longer.

This will lead to one of two results. Either the manipulator will realize that what they did is wrong and hurtful to you, and they will stop their manipulative ways or they will leave because they no longer have control. Do not be afraid of either outcome as this will strengthen your relationship with yourself, and that is the most important one you have.

Performing these steps can be very difficult and you may need the help of a therapist or a psychologist. Do not be afraid to ask for help! Sometimes manipulators know what they're doing but they don't realize it's hurting their relationship with you. If they're confronted with a calm and friendly environment in a therapist's office, things might go better.

Can You Successfully Deal With A Manipulative Partner?

As we just mentioned not every relationship needs to end because of a manipulator, although in several cases it is the best choice. One thing that you really need to remember is that even in a normal, healthy relationship it is natural to be influenced by your partner. Relationships are known to change both parties, as you grow and discover who you are together as a team. What you need to watch out for though is where you start to feel like you are losing yourself in the relationship. Your partner should be bringing the best out in you, not overpowering every aspect of your life.

We mentioned some specific ways that you can deal with manipulation in a relationship earlier in this chapter, so now we are going to look at manipulation in general. Here we are going to talk about what signs to look for to know if it is manipulation you are dealing with in your current relationship.

Understanding Manipulation

Manipulation can present itself in a variety of forms, as we discussed earlier in this book there are four main types of manipulators. In relationships though manipulation can present itself a little differently as it can be in the form of teasing and sarcasm. With how many different ways manipulation can be presented it is often very difficult to determine whether or not your partner is manipulating you.

Signs of Manipulation

many times in relationships you will start to feel like you are being manipulated, but sometimes you can't pinpoint why you feel that way. In most cases you feel that way because you aren't listening to your gut, you are going against those feelings so you start to feel a bit uncomfortable. Other times you will make decisions because of things your partner suggests, they work on getting you around to their way of thinking very subtly.

However, in order to say without a doubt that you are being manipulated you have to look at your partner's behaviors logically. You cannot go on gut instinct alone. One way to do this is to be 100% honest with yourself. Look at your partner's behavior towards you and think about what you would tell a friend if it was happening to them. If you would tell your friend to leave the relationship because the behavior is too controlling, you need to follow your own advice. If you would honestly tell them they are overreacting, chances are you are too.

What To Do If you Are Being Manipulated

Now if after an honest evaluation you have determined you are being manipulated by your partner you have a few different options. One is to leave them, which we covered how to do that in the previous chapter of this book. Your next option is to simply deal with the manipulation as we discussed in this chapter. However, you can also approach your partner to see if you can get the manipulation to stop. Sometimes partners don't even realize they are doing it.

If you decide to approach your partner you are going to want to make sure that you have a plan in place. Having a plan in place is important because sometimes confronting the manipulative person causes further manipulation. So to prevent this from happening carefully think about how you want to handle the situation, you can even use some of the approaches already mentioned in this chapter to help you deal with it.

When you do approach your partner do not do so in an accusatory manner. Accusing them only sets them on edge and can cause the entire conversation to go awry. Instead focus on the way that you are feeling rather than putting the focus on how your partner is acting. To keep the focus on you and your feelings use plenty of "I" statements. These kinds of statements will also help provide examples to your partner of what has been going on. Going this route will help open up the conversations and will hopefully prevent your partner from becoming defensive.

Now once you start the conversation with your partner you have to be willing to carry it out. You cannot go into the conversation and state your case and then just walk away. You need to listen to what your partner has to say as well. In fact, how your partner responds to your conversation is going to be what determines if the problem can be solved. If your partner accepts responsibility for what they have done chances are the problem can be solved, but both parties will need to continue to work on improving communication.

If your partner belittles your feelings or brushes you off, you need to rethink the entire relationship. Only you can make the decision of whether or not the relationship is worth saving.

No matter what you decide you still need to continue to be aware of how others are treating you. It's all too easy to get back into the same routine of manipulation. If you do stay with your partner to work things out sharing how you are really feeling on a regular basis is very important. Effectively communicating with your partner can help prevent both of you from falling into old patterns.

Chapter Seven – Raising your Self-Esteem Levels

All of the aforementioned reasons a manipulator chooses a victim are related to self-esteem levels of the victim. It's very easy to fall into a pattern of nitpicking at everything we do wrong. I'll give you a personal example.

A few months ago I missed a deadline with a client at work and I felt terrible about it. Meanwhile, I had been doing awesome with other projects and excelling in areas that I never thought I would excel in, but that one missed deadline seemed to drag me down. The rest of my projects suffered and I ended up missing more due to my lack of motivation and ultimately, the low self-esteem I was beginning to suffer from due to stress. It doesn't take much to drag a person down in today's rough and tumble economy where we're constantly competing for jobs, love, and respect.

That's why it's extremely important to follow some of these steps to keep your self-esteem boosted that you are in a better position to defend yourself against the ruthless manipulators out there who want to drag you down.

Thirteen Ways to Boost Your Self-Esteem

These thirteen ways will help you boost your self-esteem levels so that you can handle the people who are attempting to manipulate you. If these do not help, I strongly suggest you see a therapist to get some more tips and discuss why you're feeling so low about yourself.

Start with Something Small

You're not going to change your outlook in just one day, so start with something small and easily obtained in order to give yourself a gentle boost in the right direction. It's like trying to clean an entire house that is stacked full of junk. You have to start somewhere, so start in the hall closet and celebrate your success. Then move on to the kitchen and keep going to each different room. Before you know it, the entire house is clean and your self-esteem has elevated.

Use Visualization and Make it Compelling

Your imagination is a very powerful tool and you should utilize it is often as possible when it comes to your self-esteem. When you imagine an outcome, make it positive and reinforcing, not doom and gloom. Take ten minutes every morning and find a quiet place in your home. Visualize how you want to be as a confident person and then write down all of those attributes you saw in yourself. By doing this, you are training your subconscious to behave the way you want to be.

Don't Underestimate the Power of Socializing

Find people who will support you no matter what and hang out with them more often. They will give you an opportunity to practice your interpersonal skills and help you see that there are other people out there who care about you. You don't need to rely on one person for your happiness.

Do Something that Frightens You

If you're afraid of going out to parties, go out to one alone and experience it to its fullest. Don't rely on someone else to hold your hand through the situation, and if you need to, practice some breathing exercises to get through it.

Do Something You're Good At

It doesn't matter what it is. It could be painting model airplanes or even crunching numbers for a budget. Do something that you know you're good at and that you will excel at so that you feel accomplished. This will boost your confidence sky high.

Have Goals

Without goals, you have no idea where you're going in life and whether or not you've accomplished something. You should always have something you're working toward and always reward yourself when you're finished with a goal. It doesn't matter if your first goal is to clean the bathroom, do it and reward yourself for taking the actionable steps to clean the bathroom. By accomplishing things and feeling good about them, we're boosting our self-esteem levels.

Helps Others Feel Good

Give others compliments when they're feeling low or teach them something they've always wanted to learn. By helping others, you're helping yourself feel wanted and productive. Just be sure that the people you're helping are not manipulators. Do not allow them to have control over the situation and always be aware of those who are trying to take advantage of you.

Get Clarity

You need to have a clear idea of where you are at your lowest on a self-esteem scale and which category you need to work on first. There are three main categories: health, relationships, and finances. Rate yourself on a scale of one to ten through those categories, and work on the one that is at its lowest point. By doing this, you will boost your self-esteem in all the other areas, too.

Have a Plan

Treat your life as if you're baking a cake. You need actionable steps in order to accomplish your goals, so make a list of small goals beneath your large one and then make a list of tasks underneath those goals. Take everything a step at a time so you don't become overwhelmed and quit prematurely. This will only hurt your self-esteem, so you have to be ready with a plan when you have a goal.

Become Motivated

It can be as simple as setting rewards for each milestone you complete underneath a goal, or it could be reading an inspirational book. We find inspiration and strengthen in others' ability to overcome hardships, so find something that really makes you want to get started.

Get External Compliments

It may seem awkward and a little odd, but go to a family member or a friend and ask them to be honest with you about your strengths and what they love about you. Sometimes we need to hear someone else tell us what we're good at, but don't rely on this too much. Take those strengths and expand on them with the knowledge you have about yourself.

Use Affirmations

Affirmations have to be used in the correct way in order to be productive and helpful. You cannot be sitting on your couch and tell yourself that you are highly motivated and productive. Instead, ask yourself why you're sitting on the couch and is this your best self? Is this what you want to be doing right now in order to be ideal? Your affirmations must be the *truth*, and not something that you want to be true. You have to be honest with yourself and take the first step toward doing something of value.

It would be empty words with no meaning if you sat down in front of a mirror and told yourself you were beautiful every morning without believing those words. You have to dig deep and find the belief that you are beautiful inside and mentally repeat it in order to make it stick.

Stop Comparing Yourself to Others

All too often we're stuck in this vicious cycle of comparing ourselves to others. We need to know what the latest fashion models are wearing so that we can emulate them. If our coworker has something that's better than what we have, well then, we must not be worthy of love or companionship. Stop looking to others for how you should feel about yourself. Just accept that you have to move at your own pace and travel your own path to becoming the person you want to be.

Chapter Eight – Following Through with Getting Rid of a Manipulator

Sometimes you fall back into your old pattern because it's familiar and humans crave familiarity. The best way to counteract this is to use self-esteem boosting techniques continuously rather than using them once and getting rid of them. In addition, you should remember some of the following steps if you're tempted to get back together with someone who has manipulated you in the past.

Avoid Contact

If you have been with someone who manipulated you in the past, the best thing to do is avoid contact with that person. Do not allow them to call, text, Facebook, or show up in places where you once frequented. In fact, change your number, Facebook, and start frequenting *other* places in order to avoid that person. This is your best bet when it comes to staying out of a manipulative relationship because it's too easy to fall back to what is familiar.

If you have to talk with this person for any reason or you end up seeing them in a public setting, take a friend with you or call one for support.

Don't Change Your Mind

You may feel sad, lonely, and just downright terrible about the relationship and how it ended, but don't be tempted to change your mind. Remember the reasons you did this. In fact, write them down so that you see them in front of you. This makes it more solid for you and helps you recall the emotional turmoil you went through before. It'll be nothing to feel a little sad every now and then compared to feeling controlled constantly.

Spend Time with Friends and Family

You should be with the ones who love you during this tough time. If you feel comfortable enough, open up to them and tell them what happened in your relationship. A confidant will be able to listen to you without judgment, and you're really going to need that during the rough road of recovery ahead.

At this point, it would be a good time to reach out to old friends or even find a support system within a therapist's office or a group. Surround yourself with people who are understanding and empathetic of your situation.

Stay Busy

If you're spending all your time alone and thinking about the relationship, you will never get past it. This doesn't mean you have to go out and party, but spend some time doing something you love like skiing or jogging. Immerse yourself in work or school for a little while.

Write down Why You're Happy

When you write down why you're out of the relationship, write down why you're happy, too. Be sure to note that you're not being controlled anymore, and this is an excellent reason to celebrate! Whenever you have a weak moment, refer back to your list and remember why you left in the first place.

Warnings About Getting Rid of a Manipulator

Getting rid of a manipulator is supposed to be a good thing, but sometimes things can go horribly wrong. While in some cases getting rid of the manipulator is as simple as walking out and not looking back, there are several manipulators out there who simply won't take no for an answer. With these kinds of people you need to be a bit more persistent, you have to stand up to them and not back down. However, standing up to them can go horribly wrong, if you don't take certain precautions.

If you have broken it off with a manipulator the last thing you want to do is continue to see that person, but what happens if they simply show up at your house, which happens more than you might think. If they do show up you need to be smart about things, don't let your emotions over run you, think things through before doing anything. If you are home alone do NOT answer the door, do NOT talk to them at all. The best thing to do is cut off all contact, even if other people are around. And most of all be consistent, don't talk to them one day, but not the next, as that can send mixed messages.

Always pay attention to your surroundings, some manipulators will revert to stalking type of behaviors. These people might threaten to harm you or they may even threaten to harm themselves. You cannot determine if the threats are serious, so what you need to do is turn it over to the authorities. If they continue to bother you, you might need to obtain a restraining order. If you do obtain one you need to call the authorities each and every time they violate it, if you give them an inch they will end up taking a mile.

In addition to contacting the authorities, if they begin stalking you or threatening you, you need to come up with a safety plan and put it into action. The worst thing that you can do is underestimate them. You might be surprised at just how far they will go to keep you. Part of having a safety plan involves never going anywhere alone, but it also involves having a safe place to stay. Don't be afraid to ask for help, your safety is far more important than your pride.

Now what you really need to keep in mind when it comes to ending a relationship with a manipulative person is that all we can offer you is advice. The advice we are giving you can backfire, so always be prepared for the worst. If you don't want to consult on expert on manipulation your best choice, as well as the safest choice, is to disengage yourself from the manipulator.

Conclusion

It's important to remember that you cannot change the manipulator, but you can change you. Learning that you have a low self-esteem can be a real eye opener and it will be hard. Dealing with that low self-esteem and boosting it up will be harder, but it's not impossible. You can change your personal relationships and change how you respond to manipulation with a little will-power, and perhaps some help from a professional.

Now is the time to take action and start building your self-esteem so that you can take on manipulators! Create a small goal for yourself, confront your manipulator, and realize that you no longer have to be a victim in this situation!

If you enjoyed reading this book and it helped you, please leave a review at your eBook provider's website.

Printed in Great Britain
by Amazon.co.uk, Ltd.,
Marston Gate.